C000111394

Published in 2012 by Helen Exley Giftbooks.
Design, selection and arrangement © Helen Exley
Creative Ltd 2012.
Copyright © Helen Exley Creative Ltd 2012.
Illustrated by Angela Kerr © Helen Exley
Creative Ltd 2012.

The moral right of the author has been asserted.

12 11 10 9 8 7 6 5 4 3 2 1

ISBN 978-1-84634-550-0

Helen Exley Giftbooks,
16 Chalk Hill, Watford, Herts
WD19 4BG, UK.

www.helenexleygiftbooks.com

A gift of
Hope

ILLUSTRATIONS BY ANGELA KERR
A HELEN EXLEY GIFTBOOK

ABOUT THIS BOOK

If you want to pursue your dreams,
this is the book for you!
Packed with 240 pages of encouraging
quotations by 142 different writers,
Hope is a gem that you will want to dip
into again and again.
You will find inspiration in the good
times and, when life gets really
difficult, you will find words of strength
and courage to make a fresh start.
A little book to recommend
to everyone you know.

BEGINNINGS

I'm filled
with joy when
the day dawns
quietly
over the roof
of the sky.

FROM AN ESKIMO SONG

*E*ach second
you can be reborn.
Each second
there can be a new
beginning. It is choice.
It is your choice.

CLEARWATER

A new life begins for us
with every second.
Let us go forward joyously
to meet it. We must press on,
whether we will or no,
and we shall walk better
with our eyes before us than
with them ever cast behind.

JEROME K. JEROME
(1859-1927)

The first sparrow of Spring! The year beginning with younger hope than ever!

HENRY DAVID THOREAU (1817-1862)

There is no medicine like hope, no incentive so great, and no tonic so powerful as expectation of something tomorrow.

ORISON SWETT MARDEN (1850-1924)

Hopeful
as the break
of day.

THOMAS BAILEY ALDRICH
(1836-1907)

*The old happiness
is withered and dead.
But, see, there is
a greenness veiling
the land...
the frail beginnings
of a new and better life.*

PAM BROWN, B.1928

Ah what adventure,
what new
beginnings await.

PETER LESLIE

*W*alk on a rainbow
trail; walk on a trail
of song, and all about
you will be beauty.
There is a way out
of every dark mist,
over a rainbow trail.

NAVAJO SONG

Each day the firs

ay: Each day a life.

DAG HAMMARSKJÖLD (1905-1961)

...A KIND OF INNER STRENGTH

I was always looking outside myself for strength and confidence but it comes from within.
It is there all the time.

ANNA FREUD (1895-1982)

*In the depth of winter,
I finally learned that
within me there lay
an invincible summer.*

ALBERT CAMUS
(1913-1960)

ALL SERIOUS DARING
STARTS FROM WITHIN.

EUDORA WELTY
(1909-2001)

*Y*ou are everything that is,
your thoughts, your
life, your dreams come true.
You are everything
you choose to be.
You are as unlimited as
the endless universe.

SHAD HELMSTETTER

L ife's challenges
are not supposed
to paralyze you, they're
supposed to help you
discover who you are.

BERNICE JOHNSON REAGON

It had been my repeated experience that when you said to life calmly and firmly but very firmly!, "I trust you; do what you must," life had an uncanny way of responding to your need.

OLGA ILYIN

I keep my ideals,
because in spite
of everything
I still believe that
people are really
good at heart.

ANNE FRANK (1929-1945)

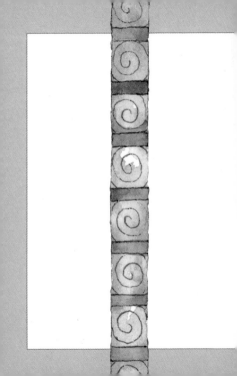

A clay pot
sitting in the sun
will always
be a clay pot.
It has to go through
the white heat
of the furnace to
become porcelain.

MILDRED WITE STOUVEN

*Hope is the thing
with feathers
That perches in the soul
And sings the tune
without the words,
And never stops
at all.*

EMILY DICKINSON
(1830-1886)

Inside myself is a place
where I live all alone
and that's where you renew
your spring that never
dries up.

PEARL S. BUCK (1892-1973)

LIFE IS
A PURE FLAME,
AND WE LIVE
BY AN
INVISIBLE SUN
WITHIN US.

SIR THOMAS BROWNE
(1605-1682)

*L*ook well
into yourself;
there is a source
of strength
which will always
spring up if
you will always
look there.

MARCUS AURELIUS
(121-80 B.C.)

DREAM!

Far away there in the sunshine
are my highest aspirations –
I may not reach them,
but I can look up and see
their beauty; believe in them...

LOUISA MAY ALCOTT

From dreams
are made the precious
and imperishable things,
whose loveliness lives on,
and does not fade.

VIRNA SHEARD

I've dreamt in my life dreams that have stayed with me ever after, and changed my ideas: they've gone through and through me, like wine through water, and altered the colour of my mind.

EMILY BRONTË (1818-1848)

Hold fast your dreams!
Within your heart
keep one still,
secret spot where dreams
may go, and sheltered so,
may thrive and grow.

LOUISE DRISCOLL

*There is a need to find
and sing our own song,
to stretch our limbs
and shake them in
a dance so wild that
nothing can roost there,
that stirs the yearning
for solitary voyage.*

BARBARA LAZEAR ASCHER,
FROM "PLAYING AFTER DARK"

Never fail yourself
Never commit to limits...
Follow
the particulars of
your spirit
as they pull you...

VERONICA D. CUNNINGHAM

WHEN YOU CEASE TO DREAM YOU CEASE TO LIVE.

MALCOLM S. FORBES
(1919-1990)

It seems to me we can never give up longing and wishing while we are thoroughly alive. There are certain things we feel to be beautiful and good, and we must hunger after them.

GEORGE ELIOT
[MARY ANN EVANS] (1819-1880),
FROM
"THE MILL ON THE FLOSS"

*I*t isn't a calamity to die
with dreams unfulfilled,
but it is a calamity not to
dream... It is not a disgrace
not to reach for the stars,
but it is a disgrace
to have no stars to reach.

BENJAMIN MAYS
(1894–1984)

Make no little plans;
they have no magic....
Make big plans,
aim high
in hope and work.

DANIEL H. BURNHAM

Hope is the dream of the waking person.

PLINY THE ELDER (23-79)

Whatever you can do, or dream you can, begin it. Boldness has genius, power and magic in it; begin it now.

JOHANN WOLFGANG VON GOETHE
(1749-1832)

Don't be afraid
of the space
between your dreams
and reality.
If you can dream it,
you can make it so.

BELVA DAVIS, B.1932

ONE PERSON
WITH A DREAM IS EQUAL
TO NINETY-NINE
WHO ONLY HAVE AN
INTEREST!

FROM "SHARE THE HOPE"

*We have enough
people who tell
it like it is —
now we could use
a few who tell
it like it can be.*

ROBERT ORBEN, B.1927

THE FUTURE BELONGS TO THOSE WHO BELIEVE IN THE BEAUTY OF THEIR DREAMS.

ELEANOR ROOSEVELT
(1884-1962)

HOPE IS THE PILLAR THAT HOLDS UP THE WORLD.

Quotation by: Pliny the Elder (23-79)

Hope is the only
good that is
common to all...
those who have
nothing else
possess hope still.

THALES (c.624-545 B.C.)

RULE
FOR
HAPPINESS:
Something to do,
Someone to love,
Something
to hope for.

IMMANUEL KANT
(1724-1804)

*If it were not for hopes,
the heart would break.*

THOMAS FULLER
(1608-1661)

Hope!...
of all ills that men endure,
The only cheap
and universal cure.

ABRAHAM COWLEY
(1618-1667)

The important
thing is not
that we can live on
hope alone,
but that life is
not worth living
without it.

HARVEY MILK

Great hopes
make great people.

THOMAS FULLER
(1608-1661)

Everything that is
done in the world is done
by hope.

MARTIN LUTHER
(1483-1546)

IN TIMES
OF TROUBLE

*The world is round
and the place which
may seem like
the end may also be
the beginning.*

IVY BAKER PRIEST
(1905-1975)

You should nurse
your dreams and protect
them through bad times
and tough times
to the sunshine
and light which
always come.

WOODROW WILSON (1856-1924)

*W*hen one door of happiness closes, another opens; but often we look so long at the closed door that we do not see the one which has been opened for us.

HELEN KELLER (1880-1968)

N
o matter how
dark things seem to be
or actually are,
raise your sights and
see the possibilities
– always see
them, for they're
always there.

NORMAN VINCENT PEALE

It is better
to light
a candle than
to curse
the darkness.

ELEANOR ROOSEVELT
(1884-1962)

We should never despair;
our situation before has
been unpromising and has
changed for the better, so
I trust it will again.

GEORGE WASHINGTON
(1732-1799)

*Only one principle
will give you courage,
that is the principle that no evil
lasts forever nor indeed
for very long.*

EPICURUS
(341-271 B.C.)

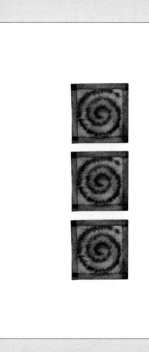

*K*eep a green tree
in your heart
and perhaps
the singing bird
will come.

CHINESE PROVERB

The shock of failure, of
disappointments, of betrayal,
hits like a physical blow.
Breathless and blinded,
you lose all contact with
the life you lived till now –
the ordinary life that seemed
untouchable. Hold fast.
However impossible it seems
that happiness and certainty
will return
– they will, they will....

PAM BROWN, B.1928

*When we are
flat on our backs
there is no way
to look but up.*

ROGER W. BABSON

Sunlight
– floating through
the whiteness

warms
the icy river
of my dreams.

JAPANESE HAIKU

*Though my soul
may set in darkness,
It will rise in
perfect light,
I have loved
stars too fondly
To be fearful
of the night.*

SARAH WILLIAMS

Be pleased

to remember that
there are bright
stars under the most
palpable clouds,
and light is never
so beautiful
as in the presence
of darkness.

HENRY VAUGHAN
(1622-1695)

O wind, If winter comes, can spring be far behind?

PERCY BYSSHE SHELLEY
(1792-1822)

*The pain passes,
but the beauty remains.*

PIERRE AUGUSTE RENOIR
(1841-1919)

OPTIMISM

*There are only
two ways to live your life.
One is as though nothing
is a miracle.
The other is as though
everything is a miracle.*

ALBERT EINSTEIN
(1879-1955)

We are all in the gutter, but some of us are looking at the stars.

OSCAR WILDE
(1854-1900),
FROM
"LADY WINDERMERE'S FAN"

The hopeful person
sees success
where others see failure,
sunshine
where others see
shadows and storm.

ORISON SWETT MARDEN
(1850-1924)

I don't think
of all the misery,
but of the beauty
that still remains.

ANNE FRANK
(1929-1945)

*When nothing
is sure, everything
is possible.*

MARGARET DRABBLE,
B.1939

I believe in the sun,
even when it is not shining.
I believe in love,
even when I do not feel it.

LINES SCRAWLED ON
A CELLAR WALL IN COLOGNE
WHICH WAS DESTROYED BY BOMBING
IN WORLD WAR II.

Keep on looking
for the bright,
bright skies;
Keep on hoping
that the sun will rise;
Keep on singing when
the whole world sighs,
And you'll get there
in the morning.

SONG LYRICS

But for me, security is not knowing what's going to happen. Because if I don't know, it could be terrific.

GLORIA STEINEM, B.1934

The way I see it,
if you want the
rainbow, you gotta put
up with the rain.

DOLLY PARTON, B.1946

I can never remember
a day in my life
when I wasn't glad
to see the morning.
There have been days
that I knew held
difficult times,
but I've never not wanted
to face the day.

GLORIA GAITHER

There is one thing which gives radiance to everything. It is the idea of something around the corner.

G.K. CHESTERTON
(1874-1936)

*No pessimist ever
discovered
the secrets of the stars,
or sailed
to an uncharted land,
or opened
a new heaven to
the human spirit.*

HELEN KELLER (1880-1968)

Hope springs eternal in the human breast.

ALEXANDER POPE (1688-1744)

O
ur way is not
soft grass,
it's a mountain path
with lots of rocks.
But it goes upwards,
forward, toward
the sun.

RUTH WESTHEIMER,
B.1928

*There isn't
a train
I wouldn't take,
no matter where
it's going.*

EDNA ST. VINCENT MILLAY
(1892-1950)

*If I knew
I should die
tomorrow,
I'd still plant
an apple tree
today.*

MARTIN LUTHER
(1483-1546)

I have always felt that the moment when first you wake up in the morning is the most wonderful of the twenty-four hours. No matter how weary or dreary you may feel, *you possess the certainty that... absolutely anything may happen....*

MONICA BALDWIN,
FROM
"I LEAP OVER THE WALL"

Every blade
of grass,
each leaf, each
separate floret
and petal,
is an inscription
speaking of hope.

RICHARD JEFFERIES
(1848-1887)

EACH DIFFICULTY MAKES US STRONGER

*You gain strength, courage,
and confidence by every
experience in which you really
stop to look fear in the face.
You are able to say to yourself,
"I lived through this horror.
I can take the next thing
that comes along."
...You must do the thing you
think you cannot do.*

ELEANOR ROOSEVELT
(1884-1962)

We ought to
remember that we
are not the only ones
to find ourselves at an
apparent impasse.
Just as a kite rises
against the wind,
even the worst

of troubles
can strengthen us.
As thousands before
us have met
the identical fate
and mastered it,
so can we!

DR. R. BRASCH

*O*ut of suffering
have emerged
the strongest souls,
the most
massive characters
are seamed with
scars....

E.H. CHAPLIN

Where there is sorrow,
where there is pain,
where there is fear –
there loving kindness grows
and flowers.

PAM BROWN, B.1928

It has never been,
and never will be easy work!
But the road that is
built in hope is more
pleasant to the traveler
than the road built
in despair, even though
they both lead to
the same destination.

MARION ZIMMER BRADLEY,
B.1930

*... we may measure
our road to wisdom
by the sorrows
we have undergone.*

BULWER

I think these difficult
times have helped me
to understand better than
before how infinitely
rich and beautiful life
is in every way and that
so many things that one
goes around worrying
about are of no
importance whatsoever.

ISAK DINESEN
[KAREN BLIXEN] (1885-1962)

*It is only when
one has been ill and has
recovered that one
can properly savour
the glory of walking,
breathing evenly,
sleeping soundly,
seeing clearly, waking
to a new day.*

PAM BROWN, B.1928

*O*ut of every crisis
comes the chance
to be reborn, to
reconceive ourselves
as individuals,
to choose the kind
of change that will
help us to grow
and to fulfil ourselves
more completely.

NENA O'NEILL

KEEP ON HOPING

The deepest prison,
sealed off from light
and sound, cannot
hold the human spirit
if hope endures.

PAM BROWN, B.1928

get into a tight
everything goes
you till it seems as
though you could not hang on
a minute longer, never give up
then, for that is just the place
and time that
the tide will turn.

HARRIET BEECHER STOWE
(1811-1896)

*H*ope *is a very*
quiet thing,
but strong.
With little sustenance,
it can endure.
With little light
it can survive.
It makes life possible.

PAM BROWN, B.1928

To endure is greater than to dare; to tire out hostile fortune; to be daunted by no difficulty; to keep heart when all have lost it – who can say this is not greatness?

WILLIAM MAKEPEACE THACKERAY
(1811-1863)

SAD SOUL,
TAKE COMFORT, NOR FORGET
THAT SUNRISE NEVER
FAILED US YET.

CELIA THAXTER (1835-1894)

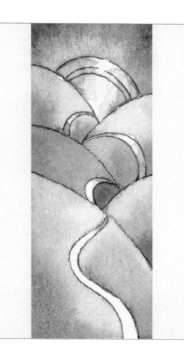

A certain amount
of opposition
is a great help...
kites rise against
and not with
the wind.

FROM "SHARE THE HOPE"

I'll match my flops with anybody's but I wouldn't have missed 'em. Flops are a part of life's menu and I've never been a girl to miss out on any of the courses.

ROSALIND RUSSELL
(1911-1976)

The glory is not in never failing, but in rising every time you fall.

CHINESE PROVERB

I long to accomplish a great and noble task, but it is my chief duty to accomplish small tasks as if they were great and noble.

HELEN KELLER (1880-1968)

*People seldom
see the halting
and painful steps by
which the most
insignificant success
is achieved....*

ANNIE SULLIVAN

All human wisdom is summed up in two words – wait and hope.

ALEXANDRE DUMAS (1824-1895)

Hope, like faith, is nothing if it is not courageous.

THORNTON WILDER
(1897-1975),
FROM "THE EIGHTH DAY"

*...I am not a quitter.
I will fight until I drop.
That is a strength that
is in my sinew....
It is just a matter of having
some faith in the fact
that as long as you
are able to draw breath
in this universe you
have a chance.*

CICELY TYSON, B.1933

Hold on; hold fast; hold out.

COMTE DE BUFFON

There are no
hopeless situations;
there are only
those who have
grown hopeless
about them.

CLARE BOOTHE LUCE
(1903-1987)

If you have hoped and your expectation was not fulfilled, then go on hoping.

THE TALMUD

Hold your head high, stick your chest out. You can make it. It gets dark sometimes but morning comes...

JESSE JACKSON, B.1941

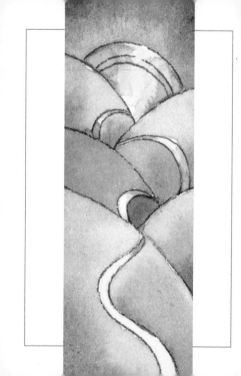

WHEN THINGS GO HORRIBLY WRONG

Our lives are like
the course of the sun.
At the darkest
moment there is
the promise of daylight.

"THE TIMES" LONDON,
DECEMBER 24, 1984

Hope is the bridge
that carries us away
from loss
and failure.

CHARLOTTE GRAY, B.1937

*S*hrug off the restraints
that you have allowed
others to place upon you.
You are limitless.
There is nothing you
cannot achieve.
There is no sadness
in life that cannot
be reversed...

CLEARWATER

THERE NEVER WAS NIGHT THAT HAD NO MORN.

DINAH MULOCK CRAIK
(1826-1887),
FROM "THE GOLDEN GATE"

The real value of ease cannot be appreciated without having known pain, nor of sweetness without having tasted bitterness, nor of good without having seen evil, nor even of life itself without having passed through death.

SADHU SUNDAR SINGH

When the heart weeps for what it has lost, the spirit laughs for what it has found.

SUFI APHORISM

*Birds sing after
a storm,
why shouldn't people
feel as free
to delight in whatever
remains to them?*

ROSE KENNEDY (1890-1995)

The darkest
despair cannot
destroy you,
so long as
there is a thread
of hope.

PAM BROWN, B.1928

*Do not fear
to hope...
Each time we
smell the autumn's
dying scent,
We know that
primrose time
will come again.*

SAMUEL TAYLOR COLERIDGE
(1772-1834)

*To lose hope is
to shut iron doors
against the light.
Allow its glow
to penetrate your
darkness and it will
give you comfort.
And strength.
And patience.*

PAM BROWN, B.1928

K eep your face
to the sunshine
and you cannot see
the shadow.

HELEN KELLER (1880-1968)

The earth is empty.
The trees, once
thick with blossom,
stand dead against
a bitter sky. The streams
are frozen.
The heart has lost
all hope. But see – along

the branches new buds
appear and greenness
pushes through
the ground unnoticed.
Spring may
be slow – but will at last
return.

PAM BROWN, B.1928

*No one
is as capable
of gratitude
as one who has
emerged from
the kingdom
of night.*

ELIE WIESEL, B.1928

Despite the sight of all the miseries which affect us and hold us by the throat we have an irrepressible instinct which bears us up.

BLAISE PASCAL (1623-1662)

The unendurable
is the beginning
of the
curve of joy.

DJUNA BARNES (1892-1982),
FROM "NIGHTWOOD"

HOPE GIVES US HAPPINESS, GIVES US STRENGTH

Hope ever urges on, and tells us tomorrow will be better.

TIBULLUS (c.54-19 B.C.)

*When the sun
is shining I can do
anything; no
mountain is too high,
no trouble too
difficult to overcome.*

WILMA RUDOLPH, B.1940

Hope is a chord,
which strikes pleasant
desires for the future;
it is everyone's sunshine,
the rainbow in
the storm, the silver lining
to the present cloud,
a star set in the
firmament of our lives....

NELLIE E. MATE

For present grief
there is always
a remedy;
however much
thou sufferest, hope;
hope is our greatest
happiness.

SCHEFER

*S*omeone once said to me,
"Reverend Schuller,
I hope you live to see all
your dreams fulfilled."
I replied, "I hope not,
because if I live and all
my dreams are
fulfilled, I'm dead."
It's unfulfilled dreams
that keep you alive.

ROBERT SCHULLER, B.1926

The natural flights
of the human mind
are not from
pleasure to
pleasure, but from
hope to hope.

SAMUEL JOHNSON
(1709-1784)

The boldest
and most ridiculous hope
has sometimes been
the cause
of extraordinary
success.

MARQUIS DE VAUVENARGUES
(1715-1747)

*...the patient's hopes
are the physician's
secret weapon.
They are the hidden
ingredients in
any prescription.*

NORMAN COUSINS
(1915-1990)

Strong hope
is a much
greater stimulant
of life than
any single
realized joy
could be.

FRIEDRICH WILHELM
NIETZSCHE
(1844-1900)

*Our hopes, though
they never happen,
yet are some
kind of happiness;
as trees, whilst they
are still growing, please
in the prospect though
they bear no fruit.*

WILLIAM WYCHERLEY
(c.1640-1716)

Hope is itself a species of happiness, and perhaps the chief happiness which this world affords....

SAMUEL JOHNSON
(1709-1784)

Hope sees the invisible, feels the intangible and achieves the impossible.

AUTHOR UNKNOWN

Hope is
a microscopic seed
from which great
things can grow
– courage and
kindness, patience,
endurance, love.

CHARLOTTE GRAY, B.1937

BELIEVE YOU CAN DO IT

You can have anything
you want if you want it
desperately enough.
You must want it
with an exuberance that
erupts through the skin
and joins the energy
that created the world.

SHEILA GRAHAM

*A*nd only when
we are no longer afraid
do we begin to live
in every experience,
painful or joyous;
to live in gratitude for
every moment,
to live abundantly.

DOROTHY THOMPSON

*J*ump into
the middle of things,
get your hands dirty;
fall flat on your face,
and then reach
for the stars.

JOAN L. CURCIO

Nothing great
was ever achieved
without enthusiasm.
The way of life
is wonderful;
it is by
abandonment.

RALPH WALDO EMERSON
(1803-1882)

*Life engenders life.
Energy creates energy.
It is by spending oneself
that one becomes rich.*

SARAH BERNHARDT
(1844-1923),
IN "MADAME SARAH"

Don't be afraid your life will end; be afraid that it will never begin.

GRACE HANSEN

If *you think*
you're too small
to have
an impact,
try going to bed
with a mosquito.

ANITA RODDICK
(1942-2007)

One doesn't
discover new lands
without consenting
to lose sight
of the shore for
a very long time.

ANDRÉ GIDE
(1869-1951)

When your bow
is broken and
your last arrow
spent, then shoot,
shoot with your
whole heart.

ZEN SAYING

*E*ach one of us
who travels further
than the obstacles
will know a
different kind of life
from that time on.

J. STONE

Learn from the past.
Do not come to the end
of your life only to find
you have not lived....

CLEARWATER

But warm, eager, living life... to learn, to desire to know, to feel, to think, to act. That is what I want. And nothing else. That is what I must try for.

GO FORWARD.
LIVE
YOUR LIFE

*Go confidently
in the direction
of your dreams!
Live the life
you've imagined.*

HENRY DAVID THOREAU
(1817-1862)

I think that wherever your journey takes you, there are new gods waiting there, with divine patience – and laughter.

SUSAN M. WATKINS,
B.1945

*B*e glad of life because
it gives you the chance
to love, to work,
to play, and to look up
at the stars.

HENRY VAN DYKE
(1852-1933)

Tomorrow
is the most important
thing in life...
Comes into us at
midnight very clean.
It's perfect when it

arrives and it
puts itself in
our hands.
It hopes we've
learned something
from yesterday.

JOHN WAYNE (1907-1979)

May you never miss
a rainbow or a sunset
because you are looking
down.

FROM
"SHARE THE HOPE"

Throw your
heart out in front
of you
And run ahead
to catch it.

ARABIC PROVERB

I *think the thing is*
always to look ahead in life,
and never look back, except
in gratitude
for happy times past.

DAPHNE DU MAURIER (1907-1989)

I avoid looking forward
or backward, and try to keep
looking upward.

CHARLOTTE BRONTË (1816-1855)

I am not interested
in the past. I am
interested in the future,
for that is where
I expect to spend
the rest of my life.

CHARLES F. KETTERING
(1876-1958)

Make voyages. Attempt them. There's nothing else.

TENNESSEE WILLIAMS
(1911-1983)

Though no one
can go back
and make a new start,
anyone
can start from now
and make
a brand new end.

CARL BARD

You have your brush,
you have your colours,
you paint PARADISE,
then in you go.

NIKOS KAZANTAKIS
(1885-1957)

Do not linger
to gather flowers
to keep them,
but walk on,
for flowers will
keep themselves
blooming
all your way.

RABINDRANATH TAGORE
(1861-1941)

*There is so much
in the world for
us all if we only
have the eyes to see it,
and the heart
to love it, and
the hand to gather
it to ourselves...*

LUCY MAUD MONTGOMERY
(1874-1942)

*Life, for all
its agonies...
is exciting and
beautiful, amusing
and artful and
endearing, full
of liking and love,
at times a poem*

and a high
adventure...
and whatever
(if anything)
is to come after it —
we shall not have
this life again.

ROSE MACAULAY
(1881-1958)

*Today is the first day
of the rest of your life.*

DALE CARNEGIE
(1888-1955)

WHEN I LOOK INTO

THE FUTURE,

IT'S SO BRIGHT

IT BURNS MY EYES.

OPRAH WINFREY, B.1954

WHAT IS A
HELEN EXLEY GIFTBOOK?

Helen Exley Giftbooks cover
the most powerful of all human
relationships: the bonds within
families and between friends,
and the themes of personal
values, peace and wisdom.
No expense is spared in making
sure that each book is as
meaningful a gift as it is possible
to create: good to give,
good to receive.

ACKNOWLEDGEMENTS:

The publishers are grateful for permission
to reproduce copyright material.
Whilst every reasonable effort has been made
to trace copyright holders,
the publishers would be pleased to hear from
any not here acknowledged.

Text: Pam Brown and Charlotte Gray:
© Helen Exley Creative Ltd. 2012.

Helen Exley Giftbooks
16 Chalk Hill, Watford, Herts, WD19 4BG, UK.

www.helenexleygiftbooks.com

ALL PICTURES BY ANGELA KERR
© Helen Exley Creative Ltd. 2012.
All words from Helen Exley's collection
of hope quotations.